Born to giggle...

Author's note:

A Journey with the Wisdom of Giggles,
to keep you smiling all day long on the hour...
Giggles are not frivolous.

As a child Holocaust survivor, the urge to write about
smiling, laughter and giggles, was the opposite of my
childhood. When I looked upward, and held my Papa's
hand, I smiled. When I saw a dog waggle his tail, I
chuckled a sort of laugh, and one day out of nowhere
came uncontrollable giggles. I felt detoxed and a bit
lighter at heart. I was grateful and looked forward to the
next time around. A Giggle here, a Giggle there, look
for their message everywhere.

And when giggles turn into hysterical laughter and every-
thing is beyond silly and funny, when you can not stop
laughing... You know you have arrived and detoxified
all unwanted Yukkkkkkkkk, physically, emotionally and
mentally.

P.S. Grace, Hope and Angel are your
Giggling angel earthly buddies,
especially when you need them the most,
they come through in a blink of a chuckle.

—e...

First edition

Library of Congress
ISBN 978-0-9987395-1-9

Published by Estherleon Schwartz

Contact: esterleon@estherleon.com
www.estherleon.com

Book and cover design and typesetting by Michael Rosen

Also by Estherleon Schwartz:
Tears of Stone and My Deal With God
Simply Meditate

Distributed by Ingram
Printed in the United States of America

*Dedicated to the miracle
of healing through laughter*

~

Simply
Meditate with Giggles

Wow,
you're beautiful

Mirrors reflect your pure soul.
AND...
now a little chuckle will create
a new day of Wow's

6AM...OMG!

Amen

believe...

believe...

believe...

7AM...Don't think, Just...

1. Brush your teeth
2. Look in the mirror and smile
3. A new fresh sight,
   a new bright day,
   ready to play
   that game of life

Hi, hi, hi, hi,

I'm Grace

Hope

I'm Angel

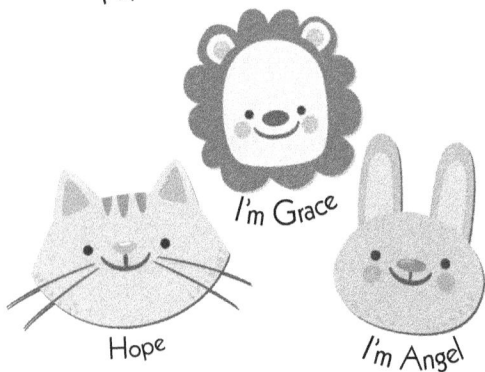

We're your invisible giggling buddies,
always at your side
We say "A Giggle a day
keeps the blues away"

Hooray!

8AM...Giggilitis is a special cure
that heals 'whatever' for sure

Start your day off
with your special smile
Giggles will follow you
after a while

Folks, give it a chance
Wiggle your lips
and let them prance to your beat
and do your dance

P.P.S...Got an
extra nickle
for a pickle, too?

P.P.P.S...That's the personality of a giggle,
to wiggle and giggle
even without a tickle
for the unexpected gift of a nickle

9AM...Giggles have their own personality

A giggle here,
a giggle there,
catch your special giggle in the air

Reach upward, it's there

P.S...Give you a nickle for your special giggle

Toodley doo
I love you, too

10AM...Selfless good deed time

Leave a piece of spinach
stuck on your front tooth
and smile

Smile big at the World
and the world can't help but
to burst into a mucho big smile
back at you
and yes, love you, too

11AM...Gigglies, Gigglies don't go away
I need you for a rainy day

Gigglies say:
Lift your eyes and heart upward
All is OK
Have a blessed day

Gigglies is following you around
Get ready for the next round
whatever, whoever comes around
Gigglies, Gigglies won't let you down

Gotcha
Thank you

12PM...A way to naturally detox
that hearty lunch

Tons of Gigglies
at brunch for lunch
And one more big giggle
to detox after lunch

Now you're ready
for more craziness
and blessings after lunch
when you're feelin' crunched

1PM...Giggles, giggles stick around
I really need your healing sound

Bring Giggling to your therapist
And say "bye, bye dude"
AND giggle, giggle
AND turn around
and really GIGGLE
that healing sound

AND
Don't look back,
Stay on track

Without a doubt
you've moved out

2PM...Put a picture in the frame
that fills your being with smiles
Those treasured memories do the same
Looking back - a ton of heartfelt miles

Wow, you're hot

3PM...When I think about giggles,
I now understand
and feel their POWER...

For me, it is soul medicine
and I feel blessed every hour

Meow, It's Hope

"Can you share a little piece
of your yummy snack
so that we can all get
back on track?"

4PM...Meow, meow,
your giggling buddie, Hope
is here to remind you

A little giggle with a yummy snack
will get your soul right back on track

Thanks

Thanks

Thanks

5PM...Make a date
and go giggling
to spread the joy of giggles everywhere

Friends that giggle together
stay together

And when their giggling ends
something inside you says, "Thanks"

AND --->

It's contagious
Go for it, Baby!

6PM...Not to worry,
Gigglies are great
to break the ice
on your 100th new date

It'll be great

AND don't be late

- Dani

7PM...You're free to giggle
because giggling is free

So take another chance for romance
and make a 101st date
let it be
to set you free

...like a force that never ends

8PM...At times giggle Gigglies
laugh and weep at the same time

Use your special sound of giggling
to ward off the gloomies
till they end

Some call it a 'beyond experience'
maybe something...

It's us...hi, hi

Grace

Hope

Angel

9PM...Mucho thanks to my devoted
secret friend,
Giggles, you are the best
in the north
in the south
in the east
in the west

I'm so grateful again and again,
for this precious gift
of Giggles from out of nowhere
that never seem to end

They're just maybe from Above

My friend, just look upward
and give some more gratitude

10PM...When everything else
temporarily doesn't work
start giggling again,
it's always ready for you

No fee, no questions
just a feeling of relief after a hearty giggle,
giggles that turn into
non-stop,
beyond-funny,
out-of-nowhere laughter
and when it stops
you feel "Wow, that was great"

WOW!

And —>

Hallelujah,
You've arrived!

11PM...When your giggles
become hysterically funny,
and uncontrollable laughter
for no reason at all...

<———

grateful

love

coffee

blessings

chocolate

doggie

peanut butter

fun

your turn!

12AM...Estherleon says:

"Keep it Simple,
Meditate with Giggles,
into a dreamy, peaceful sleep,
maybe even..."

1AM...Maybe count those soulful, loving, cutie pie, furry sheep

2AM...Give yourself and Giggles a rest
Give them a blessing
They've done their best

Just like you
you gave your best

3AM...If you awake
look upward and smile

Give thanks you've slept
for a while

Go back to sleep
and count some more
of those adorable starry eyed sheep

You!

4AM...Mirror, mirror, on the wall
Who's the fairest of them all?

...to begin a beautiful new day

with meaning and purpose

Meow, meow
Woof, woof
We love you, now go on your way,
It's a Brand new Day
Hooray!

Love, your giggling buddies,
Hope, Grace and Angel

5AM...May the source of giggles
be with you...

Author's note:

Estherleon says...
"Lift your eyes and heart upward.
Give thanks, thanks, thanks.
A calm, like after the storm
will fill every atom in your body
with more calm and joy,
to share with all those around you and more.

Yes, after my own experience with Giggles, as
I stated in the beginning of this book, I am so
happy to have shared this little pocket book
with you at your side all day long - that *Simply
Meditate with Giggles* is one unexplainable
magical cure to a broken heart and world, that
your simple smile that turns into laughter and
giggles, is medicine for this precious world."

Upcoming:

Simply Meditate
with your Dog
& Meow, Meow

Thank you so much, Ivor, for always listening.
One creative thought from you
guides me in the process.

—— e

www.ingramcontent.com/pod-product-compliance
Lightning Source LLC
Chambersburg PA
CBHW021225020426
42331CB00003B/468